This book belongs to

Ruben Lal

This book is dedicated to my children - Mikey, Kobe, and Jojo.

Copyright © 2022 Grow Grit Press LLC. All rights reserved. No part of this book may be reproduced in any form without permission in writing from the publisher. Please send bulk order requests to growgritpress@gmail.com

Paperback ISBN: 978-1-63731-314-5
Hardcover ISBN: 978-1-63731-316-9
eBook ISBN: 978-1-63731-315-2

Ninja Life Hacks™

Printed and bound in the USA.
NinjaLifeHacks.tv

When ninjas go to Europe,
There's so much fun in store.
They explore, they take photos,
Find time to play, and more!

They plan all their trip details,
For every single day –
What plane to take, what sights to see,
Where they're going to stay.

# CHECK IN →

When they arrive at the airport,
They're always first in line.
And they're very, **very** happy,
When the plane leaves on time.

The first stop is Paris,
To see the Eiffel Tower.
They're not picky at lunch
Because **veggies** give ninjas power!

Next stop on the ninja tour?
The Colosseum in Rome.
And acting out a battle scene,
Make ninjas feel at home.

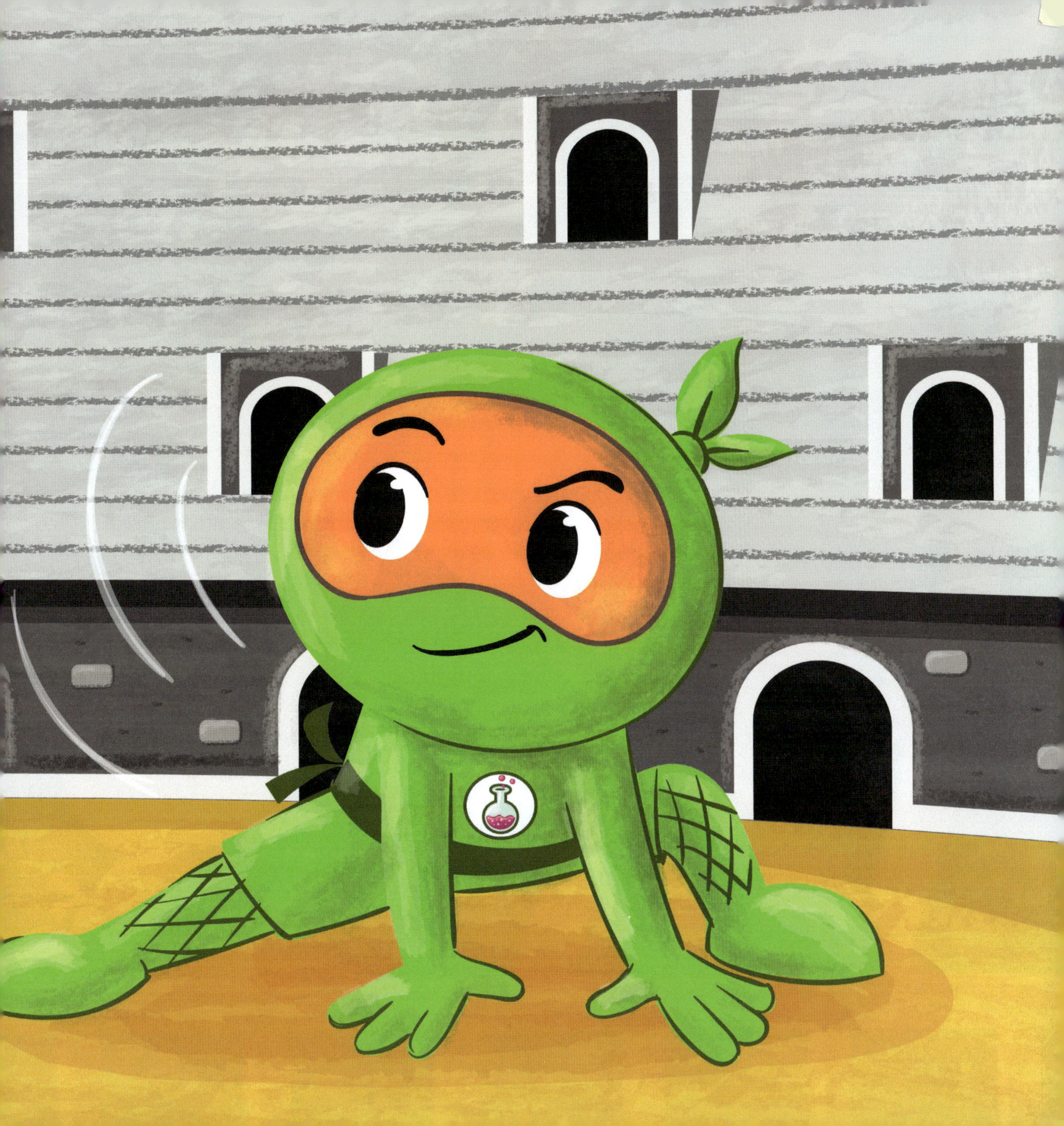

Venice is delightful,
To have a gondola ride.
And in a game of hide and seek,
Ninjas love to **hide**!

When things don't go to schedule,
Ninjas start to fret.

But ninjas know a secret...
Now you will know it too.
Not everything will go to plan, but...
There's something you can do.

Suddenly the plane takes off.
Madeira Island lies ahead.
The glassy water looks so smooth,
Near the sand that's black instead.

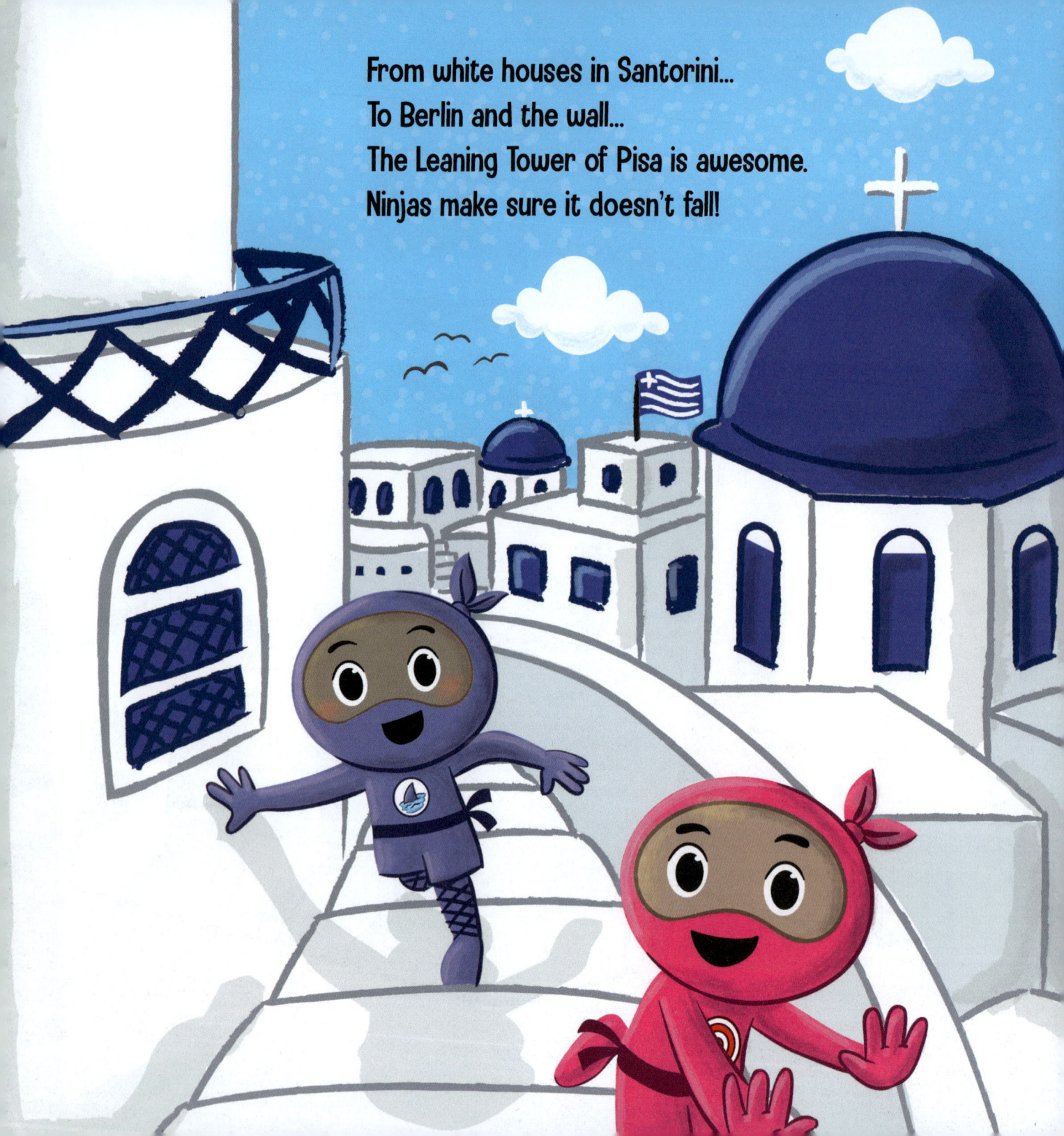

From white houses in Santorini...
To Berlin and the wall...
The Leaning Tower of Pisa is awesome.
Ninjas make sure it doesn't fall!

And now it's time to head home.
The trip to Europe is done!
But when ninjas have the travel bug,
The fun has just begun!

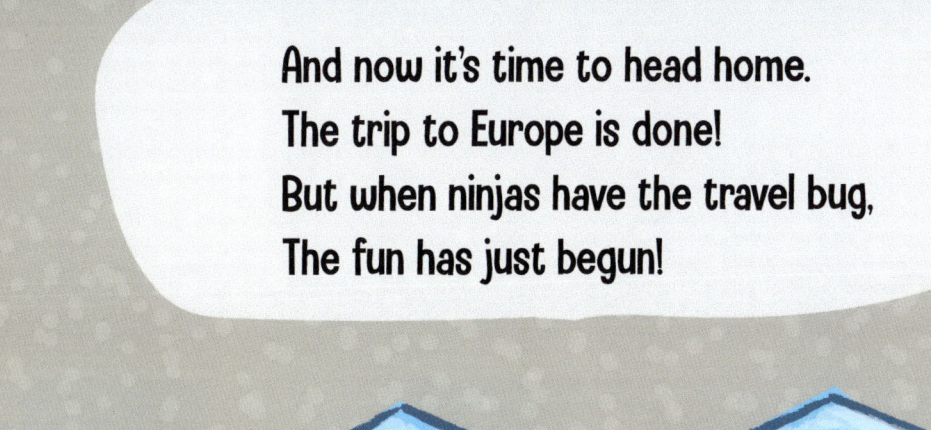

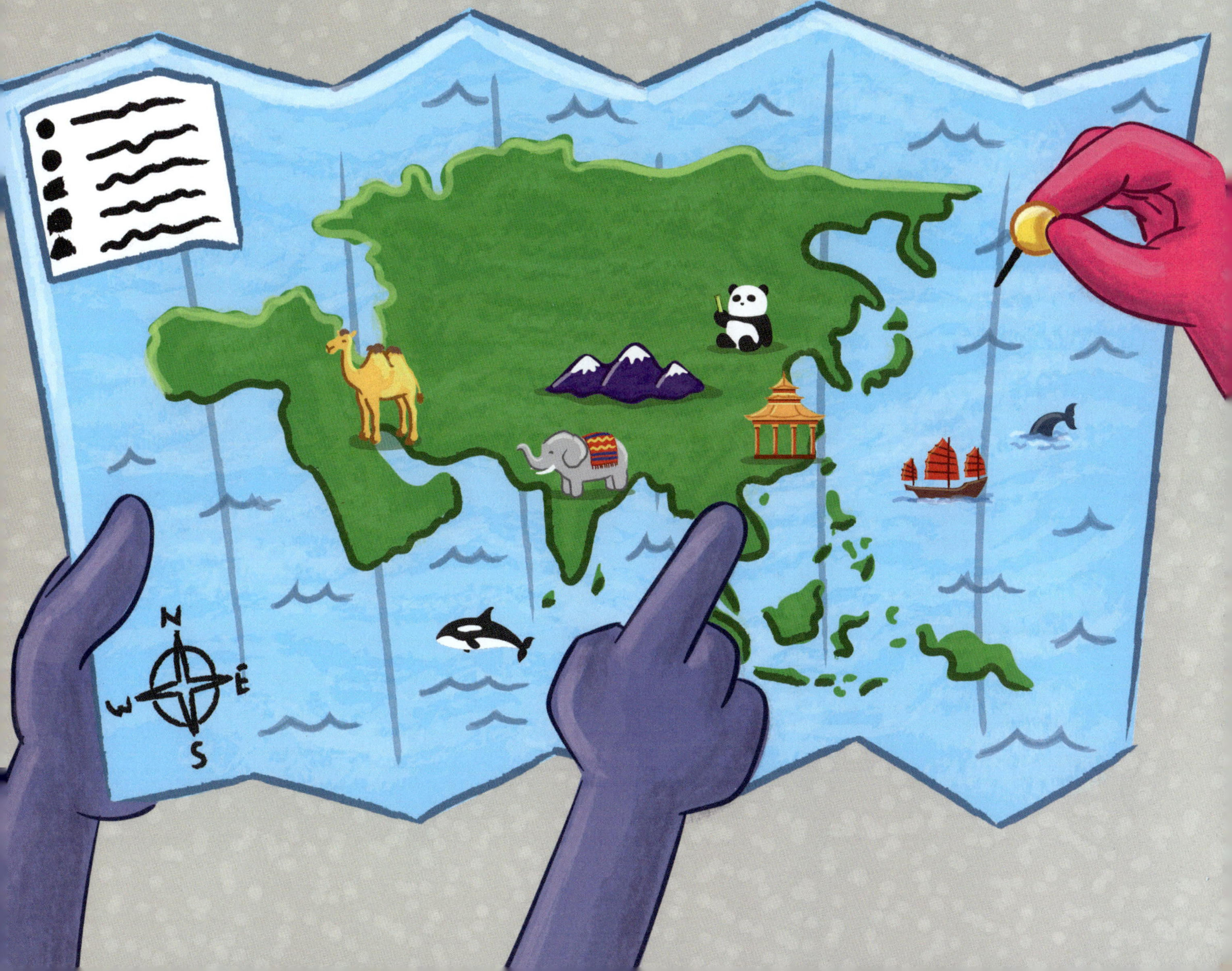

Download your beyond the book resources at NinjaLifeHacks.tv

  @marynhin  @GrowGrit
#NinjaLifeHacks

 Ninja Life Hacks

Mary Nhin   Ninja Life Hacks

 @ninjalifehacks.tv

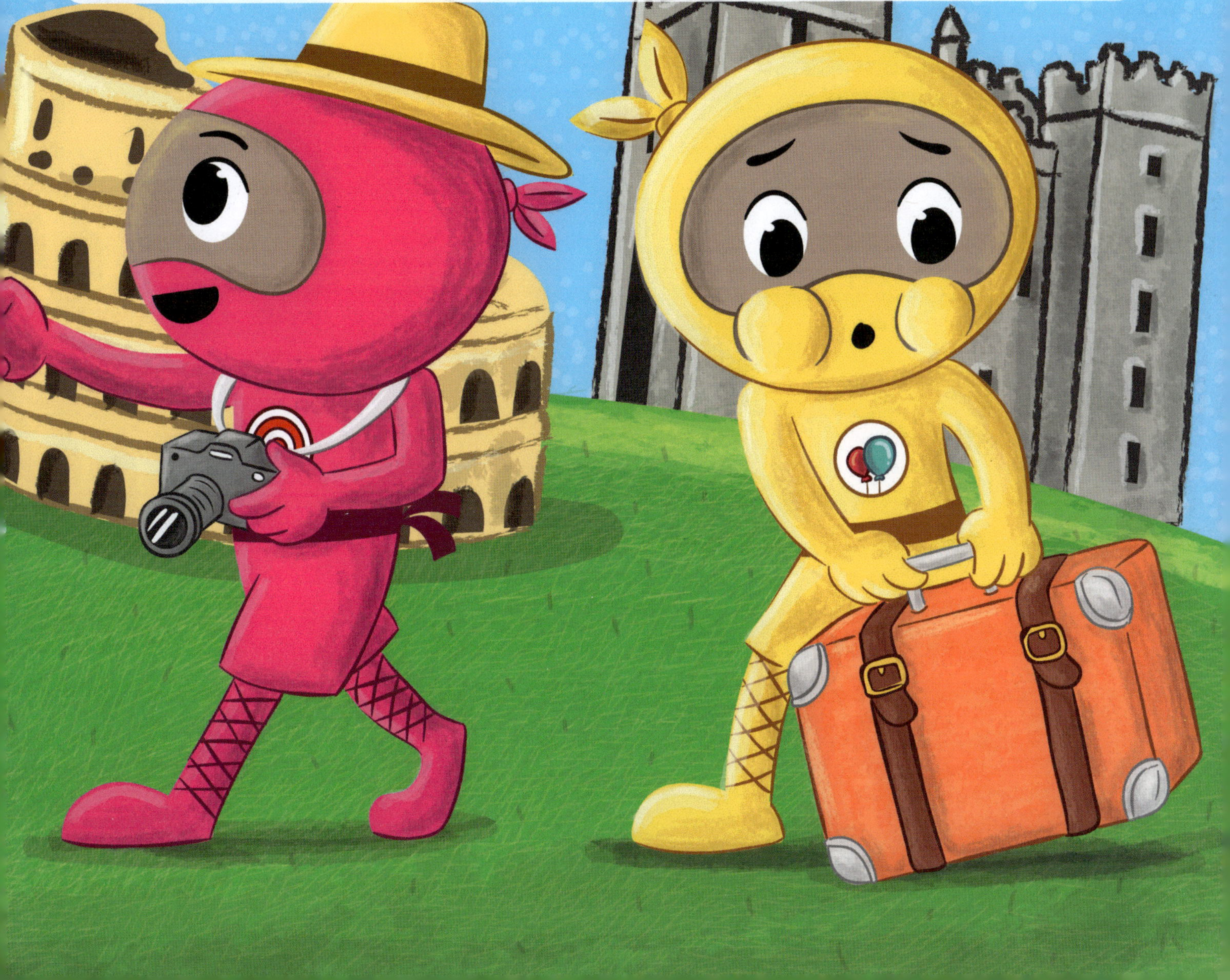

Printed in Great Britain
by Amazon